A Guide To

Figurative Language

for the development of writing skills

and also for

preparation for the 11+ Selection Tests

By Elaine C. R. Heckingbottom

This book is dedicated to the former students and staff of St Hilda's School, Westcliff on Sea – my extended family.

It is also dedicated to all those children who study with Heckingbottom Learning Ltd.; particularly for 11+ preparation in the Essex (CSSE) area. Hopefully, it will help you to get those one or two extra marks that will lift your score comfortably beyond the magic '303' that you are targeting.

Good luck to you all!

Table of Contents

Contents

What Exactly is Figurative Language?

As a painter uses brushes and paint to create an image, a photographer uses a camera, a writer also has tools to create an effect.

For a writer, figurative language is language that is used to enable words and ideas to create mental images and give impressions. When we use figurative language in our poetry and descriptive writing, it gives our ideas strength and helps the reader to understand what we mean. We can use it to enhance descriptive writing, particularly in a poetic way, by giving a more detailed picture of the object, person or place that is being described.

Figurative Language consists mainly of metaphors, similes, personification, pathetic fallacy, onomatopoeia, alliteration, idioms, hyperbole and oxymoron.

A good command of figurative language will help to build your writing skills, improving your descriptive writing and making your written work far more interesting for your audience to read.

For those of you who are preparing for the 11+ selection tests in the UK, figurative language currently features in a range of at least 2 or 3 questions in many of the English papers that feature in the 11+; however, because it is reasonably easy to grasp, it is worth working on for the possibility of a couple of 'free' marks. It is also well worth knowing these to help you with the ESPG test that features in the current Key Stage 2 SATs.

The best way to explore these different ideas is to research it. After working through each section of this short e-book, look on-line for some more classic examples, and try to understand them.

You might like to use a notebook to jot down your answers to the questions that appear through the book; or to have a go at some of the exercises that you will come across as you work through the various sections.

Once you have worked through the sections, there are a few practice questions to have a go at. These include fairly detailed explanations to help you to understand the answers more clearly.

Metaphors and Similes

Metaphors and similes are very closely related; in fact the same description can often be used in both formats.

Quite basically, a metaphor IS, whereas a simile is LIKE.

Look at these examples to help you.

His room is a pigsty (metaphor)

His room is like a pigsty (simile)

His room is as messy as a pigsty (simile)

His room is similar to a pigsty (simile)

Life is like a box of chocolates (simile)

Life is a box of chocolates (metaphor)

My life is an open book (metaphor)

My life is like an open book (simile)

That baby is as cute as a button! (Simile)

Metaphors

A metaphor says that something actually IS something totally different – something that it could not possibly be.

It is a comparison between two things that both share a common characteristic. One thing is equal to another because it has this characteristic.

For example, take the phrase "You are my sunshine." Just like the sun brings warmth and happiness to someone's day; you do the same, by bringing happiness to someone's day. You are sunshine because you and sunshine share the same characteristic of being able to make someone happy.

A metaphor is a much stronger image than a simile; it makes the reader feel or see something to help them understand it. It states that something is actually equal to something else; rather than being merely a comparison between two things.

Metaphors are written to create an impact on the reader. They should inspire and help people to understand the importance of something. For example, if I say "My little brother is a pig when he eats," it gives the reader a strong visual of how messy my brother is when he eats. This is very important not only in a story or poem, but in everyday conversation.

When friends came to stay with me recently, I was warned that their teenage son had a stomach that was a black hole! Immediately, I knew that it was important to have plenty of food in the house! If they had just said that his stomach was big or that he ate a lot, I wouldn't have thought that I would have needed as much food. After all, if his stomach truly were a black hole you would need a never ending supply of food!

It is important to understand how a metaphor works and to know when you have heard one. They are meant to create a vivid picture - to be a profound saying. The stronger the metaphor is, the better your ideas and intentions will be received!

Here are some examples:

- The moon is a silver coin emerging from a black velvet purse.

- A blanket of snow covered the ground.

- The test was a walk in the park.

- My father is a dragon; my mother is a mouse.

- The exam hall was a prison: their sentence – interminable.

- Life is a rollercoaster.

- Words are the weapons with which we wound those around us.

- The alligator's teeth were white daggers.

- The lake was a mirror.

How many more can you think of?

Now look at this phrase adapted from another book by the same author:

'The caretaker lived like a crab in a dark cave by the front door and only scuttled out to sweep the entrance.'

<u>Simile:</u> The caretaker lived *like a crab*

Notice the way he is later described as having 'scuttled', which enhances the simile further.

- What is the key word that shows you that this is a simile?
- Now close your eyes and try to picture this.
- Is it an effective description? In what way?

<u>Metaphor:</u> *lived ... in a dark cave by the front door.*

Clearly, he did not actually live in a dark cave ... he must have lived in a room.

What does the use of the word 'cave' tell you about the room he lived in?

Try to draw the caretaker and his room from the little information that you have been given. Do you find it effective?

Similes or metaphors?

1. As slippery as an eel.

2. He was a lion in battle.

3. She is as pretty as a picture.

4. The shop was a gold mine!

5. The clouds are fluffy, like cotton wool.

6. The striker was a goal machine.

Similes or metaphors?

1. As slippery as an eel. – simile - as

2. He was a lion in battle. – metaphor – he was!

3. She is as pretty as a picture. – simile - as

4. The shop was a gold mine! – Metaphor – it was.

5. The clouds are fluffy, like cotton wool. – Simile - like

6. The striker was a goal machine. – Metaphor – he was.

Creating Metaphors

Metaphors are trickier than similes, because you have to be very careful not to use words such as 'like' or 'as'. You have to say that something IS something different.

E.g. My little sister is a monkey; Our classroom is a zoo.

1. The teacher said 'James is a clown'. What did she mean by that?

2. Mum said 'Maria is such an angel'. What do you think she meant?

3. What metaphor could you write for someone who is a very fast runner?

4. What metaphor could you use to describe a very clever person?

5. What metaphor could you use to describe the blossom on a tree?

6. What metaphor could you use to describe your teacher?

7. Can you think of a metaphor to describe your pet or another animal?

8. Can you think of a metaphor to describe the sun?

Creating Similes

Similes are a little easier, because you get to use words such as 'like' or 'as'.

Can you complete these similes? Try to use four or more words of your own each time, rather than just a single word.

1. As happy as ...

2. As quiet as ...

3. As lonely as ...

4. As dark as ...

5. As clever as ...

6. As sleepy as ...

7. As quick as ...

8. As fast as ...

9. As fit as ...

10. As sober as ...

See if you can think of a great simile to describe...

1. Your best friend

   My best friend is like ...

   My best friend is as ...

2. Your teacher

3. Your pet or another animal

4. An elephant's ears or its trunk

5. Your parents

6. A sunny day

7. A wintery day

8. A tree in springtime

9. A tree in the autumn (think of the colours of autumn, and autumn festivals such as bonfire night to help you here!)

10. A tree in the winter

Can you turn any of your similes into metaphors now?

Personification and Pathetic Fallacy

Personification and pathetic fallacy are very closely linked, as they both relate to likening inanimate objects or aspects of nature to people. The difference is that one relates to how things may be described as <u>acting</u> or <u>behaving</u>; whilst the other relates to how they might be <u>feeling</u>.

Personification

Personification is saying that an inanimate object or an aspect of nature acts in a way that a person might act.

Here are some examples:

- The autumn leaves waved goodbye to their parent trees and danced to the ground;
- The sun smiled down;
- The waves frolicked and beckoned me in.
- The door yawned, beaming its friendly welcome to the visitors and encouraging them to enter.
- The moon smiled.
- The wind wrapped itself around my face.
- Death had come for her.
- The alarm clock screamed at me this morning.

This is a poem by a famous poet called Sylvia Plath.

I am silver and exact.

I have no preconceptions.

Whatever I see I swallow immediately

Just as it is, un-misted by love or dislike.

I am not cruel, only truthful.

Can you work out what it is about? Look it up on Google if you are unsure!

Can you see how personification has been used in it?

Pathetic Fallacy

Pathetic Fallacy is a form of personification; however, it is saying that an inanimate (non-moving) object or an aspect of nature has feelings or emotions.

The feelings or emotions that they are given will usually relate to something else that is happening around them.

Here are some examples:

- The flowers looked sad in the lonely room.
- The angry waves bashed the shore.
- The sad, bare trees mourned the loss of their leaves.
- The miserable pencil scratched the surface of the paper leaving a dismal trail behind it.
- Joyfully, the yellow pencil coloured in the sun.
- The sky cried morosely.
- The cheerful flowers smiled welcomingly from their plastic wrapper.

Look at the example that you have been given and see if it relates to actions (what the thing is supposed to be doing) or feelings to help you to decide here.

Think to yourself: How can flowers be happy? How can the sun be sad or happy? How can clouds be miserable or morose? That's pathetic – it's a pathetic fallacy!

<u>Over to you</u>

Try these – are they personification or pathetic fallacy?

1. The friendly sun smiled from between the sullen clouds.

2. Peggy heard the last piece of cheesecake in the refrigerator calling her name.

3. The sorry engine wheezed its death cough.

4. The sky wept miserably as the leaves fell from the trees.

5. The sunshine threw the man's hat away.

6. Sullen clouds gloomily hid the sun's cheerful face.

7. The candle flames danced in the darkness.

8. The candles sparkled cheerfully, brightening the darkness of the room.

<u>Answers</u>

1. The friendly sun smiled out from between the sullen clouds.

   Pathetic Fallacy – how can the sun be friendly, and how can clouds be sullen?

2. Peggy heard the last piece of cheesecake in the refrigerator calling her name.

   Personification – an action is being described here

3. The sorry engine wheezed its death cough.

   Personification – an action is being described

4. The sky wept miserably as the leaves fell from the trees.

   Pathetic fallacy – Although the sky is weeping, it is being given feelings of misery which relate to things that are happening around.

5. The sunshine threw the man's hat away.

   Personification – look at the action involved!

6. Sullen clouds gloomily hid the sun's cheerful face.

   Pathetic fallacy. The clouds and the sun have both been given feelings.

7. The candle flames danced in the darkness.

   Personification – the flames are described as dancing.

8. The candles sparkled cheerfully, brightening the darkness of the room.

   Pathetic Fallacy – look at the emotions that are given.

How much personification can you spot in this short poem about a house in the morning?

Can you spot any examples of pathetic fallacy?

Slowly, the house awakens,

Sleepily stretching its chimneys to greet the sun.

Downstairs, the door yawns ajar,

Smiling its cheerful welcome to the passers-by.

The curtains blink open,

Allowing the rooms to peer out through their eye-like windows,

Appreciating the dawn of a brand new day.

Examining Personification

Which word gives the quality of a person?

1) The sun stretches its warmth across the land.

2) The chair danced as the baby bounced to and fro.

3) The darkness wrapped its arms around me.

What does this tell you and how do you feel?

1) The wind sang her mournful song through the falling leaves.

2) The video camera observed the whole scene.

3) The rain kissed my cheeks as it fell.

4) The daffodils nodded their yellow heads at the walkers.

5) The water beckoned invitingly to the hot swimmers.

6) The china danced on the shelves during the earthquake.

7) The car engine coughed and spluttered when it started during the blizzard.

Using Personification as a tool

Personification is a reasonably easy tool to use to enhance a description. Take an object and try to picture yourself as that object, imagining yourself moving like it. What could you say you were doing?

For example, if you were a pencil, writing or drawing, you could be dancing across the page; you could be walking across the page, you could even be leaving tears on the page etc.

With food, it could call to you; whisper your name temptingly; shout at you; demand you to eat it. What else can they do or say?

Can you think of your own example of personification for leaves falling to the ground from the tree?

There are some examples on the next page – see how they fit with your ideas.

Examples of personification – pencils, food and leaves.

- The pencil danced across the page, leaving its footprints on the paper.

- The pencil twirled its way across the page.

- The fudge bar whispered my name, tempting me to eat it.

- The ice cream was calling to me from across the room. How could I resist it?

- The chocolate beckoned to me, temptingly, encouragingly. What could I do but obey?

- The leaves danced to the ground.

- The leaves hopped off the tree.

- The leaves waved goodbye to the tree.

- The leaves cried out in pain as they fell from the tree.

Can you use personification to describe the actions of some of the following?

A door	The waves
The sun	Flowers in a vase
A fire	A house in the morning
A tree	A book
A sandy beach	A car

Can you give any of them feelings to add a bit of pathetic fallacy?

Can you think of anything else that you could use personification to describe?

Alliteration

Alliteration (or a-letter-ation) is a tool that you have probably used many times through your primary school career – particularly in poetic writing. It is where two or more words in a short phrase or sentence begin with the same letter; however, please note:

- Not every word must be alliterative. You can use prepositions, such as off and pronouns such as his and hers; and still maintain the alliterative effect.
- Alliteration does not need to be an entire sentence. Any two-word phrase can be alliterative.

A few years ago, the text used for the CSSE English Paper was Captain Corelli's Mandolin. This included a weak example of alliteration that caught a lot of people out, because there were only two alliterative words and they were not next to one another: '...*added to the cacophony of cascading pans and dishes...*'

Don't forget to watch out for examples like this!

Adventures With Alliteration!

Alliteration Zoo

Can you create a 2 or 3 word phrase for each letter of the alphabet, using the name of an animal as your key word?

E.g.   Angry, ambitious albatross

        Brusque, boisterous badgers

Adjective/Noun Alliteration

Add a noun to each of these adjectives to create an alliterative phrase. Can you add an additional adjective as well?

1) purple
2) cosy
3) soft
4) happy
5) gentle
6) empty
7) tired
8) awesome
9) wonderful
10) circular
11) ugly

Alliterative Phrases

Write an alliterative phrase for each letter below.

1. B

2. K

3. Q

4. I

5. N

Choose a letter at random and use that to start each sentence.

My name is …

My best friend is …

We like …

e.g. My name is Jane

My friend is Joanne

We like jiving juicing and gymnastics!

(Yes – this is alliterative because they all start with the same sound – j)

Try creating an alliterative tongue twister!

- Peter Piper Picked a Peck of Pickled Pepper

- She sold sea shells on the sea shore. (2 alliterative sounds in this one – 'sh' and 's'!)

What can you create?

Alliterative Phrases 2

Remember, a true alliterative phrase only needs 2 or 3 words that start with the same sound blend and are close together,

- A cacophony of collapsing saucepans and casseroles
- Wriggling and writhing like serpents
- A cosy, cuddly kitten curled into a tiny ball.

Can you create an alliterative phrase to describe …?

- A tree
- A leaf
- An elephant
- A banana
- A peach
- A monster
- A member of your family
- Your bedroom
- Your classroom

Onomatopoeia

These are words that sound like the noise that they represent; e.g. bang, crash, pop, drip etc.

The word 'onomatopoeia' comes from the combination of two Greek words, one meaning 'name' and the other meaning 'I make,' so onomatopoeia literally means 'the name (or sound) I make.' In other words, the word means nothing more than the sound it makes! The word 'Boing,' for example, means nothing more than its sound. Basically, it is only a sound effect.

Onomatopoeic words are usually used to describe 5 specific categories of words:

- Words related to water such as burble, gurgle, drip and drop etc.

- Words related to the voice such as giggle, growl, grunt, mutter etc.

- Words related to collisions such as bang, crash, thump etc.

- Words relating to the air such as flutter, whisper, fizzle etc.

- Words relating to animal sounds such as woof, neigh, meow, baa etc.

Reviewing examples of onomatopoeic words and their various sound categories is an excellent way to learn to recognize and understand onomatopoeic words. Look for the patterns that almost always exist, and if you ever have a question about what an onomatopoeic word means, just ask yourself, 'What does it sound like?'

Look up the word 'sibilance' – a fantastically onomatopoeic word.

- I could hear the sibilance of the water sprinklers all around me.
- The sibilance of the kettle was like an angry snake.

A classic example of this is the quote from 'It Shouldn't Happen to a Vet' by James Herriot. He is about to treat a dog, and is wondering whether he should take its temperature by inserting a thermometer up its rectum when he states that "...again I heard the low booming drum roll..."

Try reading it aloud and listening for the sounds!

Needless to say, he values his fingers and does not take the dog's temperature!

Animal sounds are frequently onomatopoeic. Think of the song 'Old MacDonald' and all the lovely onomatopoeic sounds in there!

- The snake hissed loudly

- The St Bernard had a very loud woof.

- Snap! The alligator's jaws closed over its prey.

Circle the onomatopoeic word.

1. The spaceman zapped the alien.

2. James gargled his mouthwash; then regretted starting his day with orange juice!

3. The dishes fell to the floor with a clatter.

4. As the soldier ran through the field, a bullet whizzed by his ear.

5. Peter had a hard time hearing the teacher over his grumbling stomach.

6. Mary was so dissatisfied with her work that she crinkled up the paper and threw it in the bin.

7. The cancer patient sounded like he was hacking up a lung as he coughed.

8. I secretly ripped up the letter that my ex-boyfriend sent me.

9. Jake was pleased when he heard the new pencil sharpener hum efficiently.

10. When he pressed on the accelerator, the car took off so quickly that his tyres screeched.

11. We all knew she was in the kitchen because the cabinet opened with a distinct creak.

12. If you're going to cough, it is always polite to cover your mouth.

13. The lion's mighty roar could be heard across the savannah; causing the zebra to flee in terror.

14. Whoosh! The race car zoomed past the finish line.

15. You could hear the slap from across the room, but the teacher did not seem to notice.

16. The clamour of the clattering and clashing of pans even woke Grandpa from his snoring!

17. Even after several months in captivity, the prisoner was still terrified to hear the crack of the whip.

18. The baby will cry if you pop his balloon; and then you will get in trouble!

19. Jane rested her head on the window pane and watched as the rain trickled down the gutter.

20. Kirsty looked away as Mrs Jones plopped a scoop of something on her tray.

21. After making a rude remark, Jade snapped her fingers and rolled her neck.

22. Having never previously left the city, Juan eagerly sniffed the country air.

23. We were all astounded when Dad released an enormous belch from the pit of his stomach

Can you write an onomatopoeic word to describe each of the following? The first one has been done for you – although you may find an alternative one!

1. A doorbell   Ding dong!   Buzz!   Brring!

2. Getting a paper cut

3. A door slamming

4. A fire engine

5. Sneezing

6. A cow on a farm

7. Tearing paper

8. A child playing

9. A horse galloping

10. Someone drinking water

11. Strong winds

12. Waves on the shore

Idioms

Idiom are phrases that give you an idiotic mind picture. They don't mean exactly what they are saying and usually have a hidden meaning but, if you look at them literally, they make you want to giggle!

> e.g. It's raining cats and dogs!
>
> He caught my eye!
>
> I'm all ears!
>
> A leopard can't change its spots!
>
> That test paper was a piece of cake!
>
> It's all Greek to me!
>
> I'm up to my ears in egg boxes!
>
> I'm drowning in paperwork!

This sort of phrase is fantastic to illustrate, but it is not always easy to work out what they really mean. Have a look at the example on the next page to see what I mean.

Over to You

Can you match these 10 idioms with their meaning from the list below? The answers are on the next page.

Idioms

1. to bury the hatchet
2. to draw the long bow
3. to mind one's p's and q's
4. to let the cat out of the bag
5. to ride the high horse
6. to hit below the belt
7. to smell a rat
8. to paddle one's own canoe
9. to blow one's own trumpet
10. to be a wet blanket

Meanings

A. to be suspicious
B. to be very arrogant or cocky
C. to be a spoilsport
D. to boast about yourself
E. to exaggerate
F. to make peace
G. to give away a secret
H. to act unfairly
I. to be careful how you behave
J. to do things for yourself

The Answers

1. to bury the hatchet = to make peace
2. to draw the long bow = to exaggerate
3. to mind one's p's and q's = to be careful how you behave
4. to let the cat out of the bag = to give away a secret
5. to ride the high horse = to be very arrogant or cocky
6. to hit below the belt = to act unfairly
7. to smell a rat = to be suspicious
8. to paddle one's own canoe = to do things for yourself
9. to blow one's own trumpet = to boast about yourself
10. to be a wet blanket = to be a spoilsport

What do you think these idioms might mean?

1. The ball's in your court!
2. Great minds think alike!
3. You are what you eat!
4. It's a small world!
5. She's so full of herself!
6. It's a piece of cake!
7. It's water under the bridge.
8. Who let the cat out of the bag!
9. I'm all ears!
10. He took everything but the kitchen sink.

Here are your options!

a. Clever people think the same.
b. Who gave away the secret?
c. It's your decision.
d. It's easy to do.
e. It's already happened so there's nothing we can do about it.
f. I'm listening attentively.
g. He took everything he could except the essentials.
h. To stay healthy, you eat healthy foods
i. You bump into people you know in unexpected places.
j. She's really boastful.

Here are the answers!

1. The ball's in your court!

    It's your decision.

2. Great minds think alike!

    Clever people think the same.

3. You are what you eat!

    To stay healthy, you eat healthy foods

4. It's a small world!

    You bump into people you know in unexpected places

5. She's so full of herself!

    She's really boastful

6. It's a piece of cake!

    It's easy to do.

7. It's water under the bridge.

    It's already happened so there's nothing we can do about it.

8. Who let the cat out of the bag!

    Who gave away the secret?

9. I'm all ears!

    I'm listening attentively.

10. He took everything but the kitchen sink.

    He took everything he could except the essentials.

See if you can find some more for yourself; and have fun illustrating them! Try drawing their literal meanings as well as their real meanings – have fun with idioms! I certainly do!

Instructions on a well-known lemon meringue pie mix tell you to cook it for 5 minutes and then 'turn into a pastry case'! I have even tried saying 'Abracadabra - you're a pastry case' – but somehow it never works! Where am I going wrong? ☺

Oxymorons

An oxymoron is a phrase where the key words seem to contradict each other. The word oxymoron comes from a combination of two Greek words that mean 'sharp dull' – which is an oxymoron in itself!

Quite often, when you hear or read an oxymoron, you will think, "That's a daft (or moronic) thing to say because those words really shouldn't go together."

Some examples include:

- She's pretty ugly.
- We made haste slowly.
- It was an awfully good play.
- I was jolly sad to see her leave.
- He did it accidentally on purpose.
- I saw him at the farewell reception.
- She's an awfully good teacher!
- It's an open secret.
- It was seriously funny!
- It was a bitter sweet moment.
- I'm cheerfully pessimistic about their results.
- The phrase was clearly misunderstood.
- That's a definite maybe!
- She was conspicuous by her absence throughout the last 2 months of term.

    etc.

You can see that there are lots of them, and they are in common use. Listen out for them!

See how many you can spot in this passage!

It was an open secret that the company had used a paid volunteer to test the plastic glasses. Although they were an original copy that looked almost exactly like a more expensive brand, the volunteer thought that they were pretty ugly and that it would be simply impossible for the general public to accept them. On hearing this feedback, the company board was clearly confused and there was a deafening silence. This was a minor crisis and the only choice was to drop the product line.

(*Much Ado About English*, Nicholas Brealey Publishing, 2006)

Answers

It was an <u>open secret</u> that the company had used a <u>paid volunteer</u> to test the <u>plastic glasses</u>. Although they were an <u>original copy</u> that looked <u>almost exactly</u> like a more expensive brand, the volunteer thought that they were <u>pretty ugly</u> and that it would be <u>simply impossible</u> for the general public to accept them. On hearing this feedback, the company board was <u>clearly confused</u> and there was a <u>deafening silence</u>. This was a <u>minor crisis</u> and the <u>only choice</u> was to drop the product line.
(*Much Ado About English*. Nicholas Brealey Publishing, 2006)

Over to You

Can you identify each oxymoron in these sentences and explain them?

1. My younger brother took the larger half of the biscuit.

2. The teacher looked up from her marking and asked the class to keep the noise to a dull roar.

3. When Amy mentioned her idea to the class, it went down like a lead balloon.

4. It was a minor miracle that no-one was hurt in the accident.

5. He is always able to give an unbiased opinion when asked politely.

6. She asked us, in a loud whisper, whether we were happy.

7. The toy company faced a friendly takeover from their neighbours.

1. My younger brother took the <u>larger half</u> of the biscuit.

2. The teacher looked up from her marking and asked the class to keep the noise to a <u>dull roar</u>.

3. When Amy mentioned her idea to the class, it went down like a <u>lead balloon</u>.

4. It was a <u>minor miracle</u> that no-one was hurt in the accident.

5. He is always able to give an <u>unbiased opinion</u> when asked politely.

6. She asked us, in a <u>loud whisper</u>, whether we were happy.

7. The toy company faced a <u>friendly takeover</u> from their neighbours.

<u>Hyperbole</u>

Hyperboles are great fun to use, because a hyperbole is an extreme exaggeration, which is not meant to be taken literally.

It comes from a Greek word meaning 'excess'

e.g.   There was a mountain of food in front of me.

         He ran as fast as the speed of light.

Often used comically, hyperboles are a fun way to spice up writing.

Other examples of hyperboles include:

- o   The soup bowl was deeper than the sea

- o   The peas were piled a mile high

- o   We had to walk miles to get from the station to the museum.

- o   I am so hungry, I could eat a horse.

Over to you

Find the hyperboles in these sentences.

- She cried a river of tears.

- When he shouted, she jumped 10 feet high!

- He was dying to go to the party.

- I've got a million things to do before I go on holiday next week!

Are these hyperboles or not?

- Mark is growing so fast, he will soon be taller than the trees.

- Maria is the tallest girl in the class.

- My rucksack weighed a tonne.

- It's raining really hard outside.

- Amy is the best mathematician in the class.

- Amy is a human calculator.

- I was so tired I could have slept for a year.

- This bag is really heavy

- My bedroom is so small; you couldn't swing a cat in there.

Find the hyperboles in these sentences.

- She cried <u>a river of tears</u>.

- When he shouted, <u>she jumped 10 feet</u> high!

- He <u>was dying</u> to go to the party.

- I've got <u>a million things to do</u> before I go on holiday next week!

Hyperboles or not?

- Mark is growing so fast, he will soon be taller than the trees. - Yes

- Maria is the tallest girl in the class. - No

- My rucksack weighed a tonne. - Yes

- It's raining really hard outside. - No

- Amy is the best mathematician in the class. – No

- Amy is a human calculator - Yes

- I was so tired I could have slept for a year. - Yes

- This bag is really heavy - No

- My bedroom is so small; you couldn't swing a cat in there. - Yes

Underline any hyperboles that you find in the following sentences. Be careful ... some of them have none!

1) I'm so hungry I could eat a whole elephant!

2) May is the nicest month of the year.

3) Her brightly coloured dress hurt his eyes.

4) Larry was such a big baby that this parents had to use bed sheets for nappies.

5) I ate all of my salad for lunch.

6) As I approached the horse, it seemed larger than it had in the pasture.

7) The roof rose up and down to the rhythm of the loud music.

8) We thought the apple pie was the best kind of dessert for the party.

9) The dog was so dirty that it had a tomato plant growing on its back.

10) There were a million replies that popped into her head

1) I'm so hungry <u>I could eat a whole elephant</u>!

2) May is the nicest month of the year.

3) Her brightly coloured dress <u>hurt his eyes</u>.

4) Larry was such a big baby that <u>his parents had to use bed sheets for nappies.</u>

5) I ate all of my salad for lunch.

6) As I approached the horse, it seemed larger than it had in the pasture.

7) The roof <u>rose up and down to the rhythm of the loud music.</u>

8) We thought the apple pie was the best kind of dessert for the party.

9) The dog was <u>so dirty that it had a tomato plant growing on its back.</u>

10) There were <u>a million replies</u> that popped into her head

Can you think of a good hyperbole to replace the underlined words in these sentences?

1. The car ride took <u>a very long time.</u>

2. We got home <u>very quickly.</u>

3. My grandfather is <u>very old</u>.

4. The dog was <u>very big.</u>

5. My suitcase is <u>extremely heavy.</u>

Below is a recount of a trip that Jane and her mother made to the supermarket. Can you add hyperboles to enhance the underlined phrases?

Jane and her mother went to the supermarket on Saturday. As they arrived at the shop, it began to <u>rain very hard.</u> When they entered the door, they were <u>quite wet.</u>

Jane selected a shopping trolley, but its wheels were not straight. <u>It wobbled as she pushed it </u>down the aisle. Her mother quickly selected the groceries on the list. While they didn't have very many items, it was still <u>very expensive</u>. They grabbed the bags of groceries, <u>which were very heavy</u>, and returned home.

Can you think of a great hyperbole to describe each of the following?

- A huge pile of snow
- A heavy book
- A deep puddle of water
- A quiet girl
- A tall building
- A freezing cold day
- A very small room

I've not given you any answers for a lot of this section – it is very much over to you!

Irony

So what is irony? Quite simply, it is the use of words that mean the opposite of what you really think, especially in order to be funny. It can also refer to a situation that is strange or funny because things happen in a way that seems to be the opposite of what you expected.

In many ways, irony can be similar to sarcasm. It also relates to a person behaving in the opposite way from that which might normally be expected.

There are 3 main types of irony: Verbal irony, situational irony and dramatic irony. Each of these is explained in more detail over the next few pages.

<u>Verbal Irony</u>

This type of irony occurs when a character says one thing but really means the opposite. This is also referred to as sarcasm!

- "Don't go overboard with the gratitude," he retorted with heavy irony.

- That cake is as soft as concrete!

- When asked if she understood the concept of irony, Jane replied "It's as clear as mud!"

- "The irony is that I thought he could help me!" she commented, sadly.

- Looking at her son's messy bedroom, Mum commented "Wow! You could win an award for cleanliness!"

- My teacher is as pleasant and relaxed as a coiled rattlesnake!

- My walk home yesterday was *only* 23 blocks!

- Oh great! It's raining and I forgot my umbrella!

- Mother: I see you ironed your shirt!

  Son: But I just dug it out of the bottom of the laundry basket!

- You and your brother are playing a computer game when you should be doing your homework. Mum looks in and says "When you've finished that important work, I have some great maths problems that you could do for recreation!"

- Lemony Snickett uses a lot of verbal irony in his books. Here is a classic example:

  'Today was a very cold and bitter day, as cold and bitter as a cup of hot chocolate; if the cup of hot chocolate had vinegar added to it and were placed in a refrigerator for several hours.

  From Lemony Snickett: The Unauthorised Autobiography by Lemony Snickett.

  (Even the title is an example of verbal irony – how can an autobiography ever be unauthorised?)

- Think about the film Shrek. There is a scene where the two characters have the following discussion:

  Donkey: Can I stay with you? Please?

  Shrek: Of course!

  Donkey: Really?

  Shrek: NO!

  Can you see the verbal irony? Shrek says one thing, but means another – but which of his 2 comments does he really mean?

Situational Irony

This type of irony occurs when what actually happens is the opposite of what is expected or appropriate.

- Titanic: The Artefact Museum is currently closed due to water damage!

- Irony is when someone writes: Your an idiot! (This is situational irony because they show themselves to be an idiot by using the wrong form of 'your'!)

- Another case of situational irony that many Police Officers enjoy is when those they arrest say "I didn't do nothing, officer!" The rule of the double negative tells us that, if they didn't do nothing, they must have done something!

- A rat infestation closes the offices of a pest control company!

- You take your umbrella to work with you every day … except the day that it rains!

- A plumber spends the day fixing faulty taps and comes home to find a leak in his bathroom!

- The fear of long words is hippopotomonstrosesquipedaliophobia.

- Someone tweets about how useless and pathetic Twitter is – or uses Facebook to complain about Facebook!

- The police station gets burgled!

- As the thief is breaking into the police station, his own house is robbed!

- The Year 6 teacher failed the Year 6 SATs test!

- The well-known author failed the Year 6 writing test!

- A fire station burns down!

- A pilot confesses to being afraid of heights!

- You run away from someone who is throwing a water balloon at you – only to fall straight into the paddling pool!

- A man needing medical assistance wanders into the road ... only to be run over by the ambulance!

Dramatic Irony

This kind of irony occurs when the audience or readers know more about the situation than the character does. You have watched a lot of dramatic irony as you have grown up – it is evident in nearly all of the Disney and Pixar films. Look back at a few and see if you can find the irony in there!

- In The Lion King, the audience is very aware of Scar's role in Mufasa's death. Simba, however, believes that it is his fault; running away and growing up in the belief that he caused his father's death.

- The apple that puts Snow White to sleep is a great form of dramatic irony, because the audience all know that her stepmother has put a spell on it – but Snow White doesn't.

- In Ratatouille, the very idea of having a rat in the kitchen is gross to many people; so having a rat who is actually a master chef is incredibly ironic.

- In the film 'Beauty and the Beast', Gaston wants to marry Belle, but she says that she doesn't deserve him. In reality, the audience knows that he is the one who doesn't deserve her!

- In Mulan, the audience knows that Mulan is a woman, but the other men in the military do not!

Here are some examples from other films.

- In the Wizard of Oz, Dorothy travels all through Oz searching for a way to return home – only to find that the shoes on her feet have the magical power that she needs in order to get home.

- Batman doesn't know that The Joker is waiting for him; but the audience does!

- In a film, the audience all know the danger in the cupboard, but the characters don't!

- The reader of the book knows that a storm is coming, but the children, playing happily in the woods, are unaware of it.

- We all know who the murderer is in the film – but the detective, who hasn't worked it out yet, asks for his/her help!

William Shakespeare was also a wizard at dramatic irony. His use of the confusion created by identical twins, or even by similar-looking fraternal twins, abounds in his comedies; and there is a lot of dramatic irony in histories such as Macbeth and Hamlet.

- In 'A Midsummer Night's Dream, think of the time when Bottom is changed and finds himself with a donkey's head – only to have Titania, the beautiful Queen of the Fairies fall in love with him! The audience all know that this is because of a spell that has been put on both of them, but the characters do not!

  How many more examples can you think of in the play? There are loads!

- In Romeo and Juliet, Romeo thinks that Juliet is dead and so commits suicide – only for her to wake up minutes later and kill herself because she is so upset over his suicide!

    There are many other examples too for those who know the play!

- In several of his plays, a person is in disguise and the other character talks with him as if he is someone else. Since this is known by the audience, it adds to the humour of the dialogue. This is a common form of dramatic irony in 'Twelfth Night' and 'The Comedy of Errors', where identical twins appear and disappear!

- In 'The Tempest', there is a lot of dramatic irony in the confusion after the shipwreck, as three different groups of characters move around the island

    Ariel contributes to the dramatic irony as he affects the inter-relationship of the characters.

- 'Macbeth' (The Scottish Play) is full of dramatic irony. One example is the fact that the audience knows that, whilst Macbeth acts loyal to Duncan, he is planning his murder all the time!

    If you know the play, how many other elements of dramatic irony can you find?

    Think of the predictions – particularly those surrounding Macbeth's death!

An example of situational irony cropped up in the 2011 CSSE (Essex) 11+ English exam based on the text of Captain Corelli's Mandolin by Louis de Bernières, where students were asked to comment on the irony of the priest's behaviour in this passage based on the earthquake at Cephalonia.

"... the preternatural stillness was suddenly broken by the wild and savage cries of the priest, who had rushed from his church and was now wheeling and spinning, his arms raised to the heavens, his eyes flashing through the grime of his face, not imploring the deity to desist, as Pelagia first supposed, but berating him. ... The forbidden words spewed out of him, all the serenity of his pious soul transformed instantaneously into contempt, and he fell to his knees, battered the earth with his fists and, his body incapable of enfolding his range, he sprang once more to his feet and punched a fist towards the sky. Tears rose to his eyes and he demanded 'Have we not loved you?...'"

From Captain Corelli's Mandolin by Louis de Bernières (1994)

The questions were as follows:

1. What did Pelagia suppose that the priest was doing?

    This caught a few people out; but those who think logically thought – 'He's a priest. What are priests supposed to do? They pray. Who do they pray to? God!

    A good answer would be: Pelagia assumed that he was praying to God for the earthquake to stop.

2. What was ironic about the way the priest was behaving?

What do priests normally do?

They worship God, they respect and honour him; they show that they love him; they pray to him.

What was the priest actually doing?

In the text, it says that he was 'not imploring the deity to desist, as Pelagia first supposed, but berating him.' This shows that he is not doing what Priests normally do – praying to God, showing him respect, praising him – but doing something totally different; totally opposite. Even if you don't understand the word 'berating', it is fairly obvious, as you read on, that he is doing something contrary to expectation and is acting angrily towards God; battering the earth was his hands and raising a fist towards heaven – he sounds pretty cross! If you look up the word 'berating', you will find that it means 'telling off'!

A good answer would be 'Priests are supposed to love God and praise him, but the priest is angry with God and is telling him off because of the earthquake. He shakes his fist at him and shows his anger with the God that he should respect'

It is rare that I give full marks in these questions!

Over the next few pages, you will find a series of examples of a range of different types of figurative language. In each case, you need to work out which type of figurative language it is an example of.

There are four groups of questions, and each one is followed by a page of answers, along with explanations to help you to understand why that is the best fit.

1. She is such an <u>eager beaver</u>.

2. The <u>moon smiled down</u> at me.

3. I think we'd better <u>agree to disagree.</u>

4. Their forward <u>is a goal machine.</u>

5. Her face was <u>as round as the moon</u>

6. Thunder crashed and lightning flashed with increasing force across the sky as <u>the angry storm became ever more furious.</u>

7. You know that <u>linguists really like languages?</u>

8. I've told you that <u>a million times</u>

1. She is such an <u>eager beaver</u>.

   Idiom – as it creates an idiotic mind picture.

2. The <u>moon smiled down</u> at me.

   Personification – the moon is represented as doing something that you or I might do.

3. I think we'd better <u>agree to disagree.</u>

   Oxymoron – it's a moronic thing to say, as the words 'agree' and 'disagree' are actually antonyms.

4. Their forward <u>is a goal machine</u>.

   Metaphor – we are saying that he IS something that he cannot possibly be – i.e. a machine!

5. Her face was <u>as round as the moon.</u>

   Simile – we are using the word 'as' to create a comparison (or a similarity)

6. Thunder crashed and lightning flashed with increasing force across the sky as <u>the angry storm became ever more furious.</u>

   Pathetic Fallacy – how can you say that the storm is angry? That's pathetic!

7. You know that <u>linguists really like languages?</u>

   Alliteration – you have 3 words that begin with the same letter within a short phrase.

8. I've told you that a million times

   Hyperbole – it's an extreme exaggeration

9. The builder gave <u>an accurate estimate.</u>

10. Life is a dream.

11. She was a tower of strength.

12. Don't let the cat out of the bag!

13. Every cloud has a silver lining

14. You could have knocked me over with a feather.

15. The sink <u>mumbled and gurgled</u> as the water ran out.

16. The candle flame sang a song in the darkness

9. The builder gave <u>an accurate estimate.</u>

    How can an estimate be accurate? An estimate is a guess, so it is only ever accurate by sheer fluke. Oxymoron!

10. Life is a dream.

    Metaphor. You are saying that it IS something that it clearly is not.

11. She was a tower of strength.

    Metaphor. You are saying that it IS something that it clearly is not.

12. Don't let the cat out of the bag!

    Idiom. It gives us an idiotic mind picture. If you let the cat out of the bag, you are giving away a secret.

13. Every cloud has a silver lining.

    Idiom. It gives us an idiotic mind picture.

14. You could have knocked me over with a feather.

    Hyperbole – it's an extreme exaggeration.

15. The sink <u>mumbled and gurgled</u> as the water ran out.

    Onomatopoeia – you are describing the sounds that it makes. The words that are being used sound very similar to the sounds that they are describing.

16. The candle flame sang a song in the darkness

    Personification. People sing songs. Candles are

    inanimate objects that cannot actually sing.

17. She entered the room as quietly as a mouse.

18. The alarm clock went off like a bomb!

17. I could hear their buzzing, so I knew there was a

bee's nest around here.

19. The ants marched home.

20. The moon is a ghostly galleon tossed upon cloudy seas.

21. The falling leaves waved a sad goodbye to the tree.

22. She crept as slowly as a snail towards the angry

teacher.

23. She's as mad as a hatter!

24. The trees whispered to each other in the darkness.

25. He's always blowing his own trumpet.

The Answers

18. She entered the room as quietly as a mouse.

    Simile – you are comparing her lack of noise to that of a mouse.

19. The alarm clock went off like a bomb!

    Simile – you are comparing the alarm clock to a bomb. Notice the use of the word 'like'.

20. I could hear their buzzing, so I knew there was a bee's nest around here.

    Onomatopoeia – 'buzzing' sounds like the noise it is describing.

21. The ants marched home.

    Personification – soldiers march. You are likening the movements of the ants to those of a soldier.

22. The moon is a ghostly galleon tossed upon cloudy seas.

    Metaphor – you re saying that something IS something that it cannot possibly be.

23. The falling leaves waved a sad goodbye to the tree.

    Personification – they are waving. This is something people do. You are not saying that they are sad, so it is not pathetic fallacy – it is their action that is described as being sad.

24. She crept as slowly as a snail towards the angry teacher.

    Simile – note the use of 'as'

25. She's as mad as a hatter!

    Simile – again, not the use of 'as'

26. The trees whispered to each other in the darkness.

    Personification – people whisper!

27. He's always blowing his own trumpet

    Idiom – it gives an idiotic mind image that doesn't reflect its true meaning.

28. The sun went to bed.

29. She ate the mountain of food greedily.

30. The frog's tongue moved like lightning.

31. The thunder growled angrily in the sky

32. The sun stretches its warmth across the land.

33. The girl zipped up her jacket.

34. The wind sang her mournful song through the falling leaves.

35. The darkness wrapped its arms around me.

36. Her brain is the size of a pea.

37. The brown grass was begging for water.

38. He pleaded for forgiveness, but her heart was as cold as iron.

The Answers

26. The sun went to bed.

Personification – people go to bed.

27. She ate the mountain of food greedily.

Hyperbole – an extreme exaggeration, not meant to be taken literally.

28. The frog's tongue moved like lightning.

Simile – notice use of the word 'like'.

29. The thunder growled angrily in the sky

Personification and pathetic fallacy.

Growled – people do that – personification.

Angrily – an emotion. How can thunder be angry? Pathetic fallacy.

30. The sun stretches its warmth across the land.

Personification – we stretch, and so the sun is being described as doing something that people do.

31. The girl zipped up her jacket.

Onomatopoeia – the word 'zip' sounds like the noise it is describing.

32. The wind sang her mournful song through the falling leaves.

Personification – the wind is being described as singing, which is something that people do.

33. The darkness wrapped its arms around me.

Personification – the darkness is being described as doing something that we might do.

34. Her brain is the size of a pea

Hyperbole – an extreme exaggeration. No-one could survive with a brain that small!

35. The brown grass was begging for water.

Personification – people beg. The grass is being described as doing something that we might do.

36. He pleaded for forgiveness, but her heart was as cold as iron.

Metaphor – we're saying that her heart was colder than it could possibly be.

37. She's a lucky lady

38. It flew as straight as an arrow.

39. Boom! The firework shot into the sky.

40. The city was Smith's forest.

41. The skyscrapers reached for the clouds.

42. The clerks and scriveners buried themselves away in their dark caves.

43. It took a million years for Max to finish his homework!

44. There was a thundering silence in the classroom once the Head Teacher walked in.

45. The eyes of the houses had been put out with bricks.

<u>Answers</u>

37. She's a lucky lady – alliteration L, L

38. It flew as straight as an arrow. – Simile – as.

39. Boom! The firework shot into the sky. – Onomatopoeia – sounds like the noise it makes.

40. The city was Smith's forest. – metaphor – it was something it never could be.

41. The skyscrapers reached for the clouds. – personification – they're doing something we do.

42. The clerks and scriveners buried themselves away in their dark caves.

    Metaphor – dark caves – their offices are described as dark caves. What ideas does that metaphor give us about the places where they worked? Cold? Damp? Dark? Miserable?

43. It took a million years for Max to finish his homework! Hyperbole – extreme exaggeration.

44. There was a thundering silence in the classroom once the Head Teacher walked in.

    Oxymoron – two words with opposite meanings.

46. The eyes of the houses had been put out with bricks. Metaphor – what are the eyes of the houses? Think carefully about it!

Other Books by the same author, also available either in Kindle or in paperback format (or both!)

- Richard's Magic Book

- Can We Play Maths Again Today, Please?

  Build Your Child's Confidence in Mathematics through Games and Activities – A Guide for Parents and other key carers.

  Three sample chapters, especially chosen for 11+ candidates, have been enclosed in the following pages of this book.

- Are We Nearly there Yet?

  A book packed with a range games and activities to play in the car – both on long journeys and on short journeys, such as the School Run.

- Fantastical Facts for Quizzical Kids (Coming Soon)

  A book of amazing facts, quizzes and trivia to amaze and interest children who have a lively and healthy interest in the world around them.

  This is also a great book to boost the General Knowledge of a child who is about to tackle the 11+

- 11+ Guide to Short Writing Tasks.

  This is recent publication, particularly important for those preparing for the 11+ in the CSSE (Essex) region, or for Independent Schools, where writing tasks are part of the Entrance Exam. It is available both as a Kindle book and also in paperback format.

- 11+ Vocabulary Booster.

  A book of activities and flashcards to help to improve your child's vocabulary before they take an 11+ test for a selective school (UK). This book includes more than 1000 11+ type vocabulary questions.

  It is also useful for anyone learning English, or preparing for any major exam towards the end of Primary education.

  A sample from this book is enclosed on the next few pages.

11+ Vocabulary Booster – Sample pages

Synonyms are words which are very close in meaning to one another – such as open and ajar; hide and conceal; sleep and doze.

Antonyms are words that are OPPOSITE in meaning to one another – such as open and closed, reveal and conceal, awake and asleep.

Look at the groups of words below and select the **TWO SYNONYMS** (words which are closest in meaning) - one from each set.

a. (perfect, cradle, moon) (sunshine, baby, faultless)

b. (splash, scrape, new) (flash, flesh, fresh)

c. (inside, extent, incense) (outside, interior, outdoors)

d. (thunder, snowstorm, hail) (sleet, blizzard, lightning)

e. (different, similar, odd) (alike, even, quiet)

f. (cease, crease, wrinkle) (stop, start, iron)

g. (solution, excuse, remedy) (lie, tell, reason)

h. (amaze, astound, maze) (fun, garden, labyrinth)

i. (drink, drank, drunk) (water, juice, intoxicated)

The answers!

a. (<u>perfect,</u> cradle, moon)   (sunshine, baby, <u>faultless</u>)

b. (splash, scrape, <u>new</u>)   (flash, flesh, <u>fresh</u>)

c. (<u>inside,</u> extent, incense) (outside, <u>interior,</u> outdoors)

d. (thunder, <u>snowstorm,</u> hail)   (sleet, <u>blizzard,</u> lightning)

e. (different, <u>similar,</u> odd) (<u>alike,</u> even, quiet)

f. (<u>cease,</u> crease, wrinkle) (<u>stop,</u> start, iron)

g. (solution, <u>excuse,</u> remedy)   (lie, tell, <u>reason</u>)

h. (amaze, astound, <u>maze</u>)   (fun, garden, <u>labyrinth</u>)

i. (drink, drank, <u>drunk</u>)   (water, juice, <u>intoxicated</u>)

<u>Notes</u>

- The opposite of interior is exterior!
- Whilst hail and sleet are relatively similar in that they are both forms of cold precipitation, snowstorm and blizzard are virtually the same.
- Drink, drank, drunk is always a funny one, especially when you look at the way the tenses work. John drinks the wine, John drank the wine; the wine was drunk (and so was John – he was intoxicated!)

Look at the groups of words below and select the **TWO** antonyms (words which are most opposite in meaning) – one from each group.

(hour, small, huge)   (minute, clock, chair)

(loud, expensive, gentle) (dear, quiet, noise)

(rear, fear, near)   (back, tear, far)

(inside, insect, incapable)   (capable, side, sect)

(swim, float, dive)   (bath, sink, toilet)

(dear, sweetheart, love) (nice, cheap, expensive)

(few, minority many)   (mostly majority certainly)

(glib timid tiresome)   (fib bold blame)

(foolish ignoramus rude) (wise known discourteous)

The Answers!

(hour, small, <u>huge</u>)   (<u>minute,</u> clock, chair)

(<u>loud</u>, expensive, gentle) (dear, <u>quiet,</u> noise)

(rear, fear, <u>near</u>)   (back, tear, <u>far</u>)

(inside, insect, <u>incapable</u>)   (<u>capable</u>, side, sect)

(swim, <u>float</u>, dive)   (bath, <u>sink</u>, toilet)

(<u>dear</u>, sweetheart, love) (nice, <u>cheap</u>, expensive)

(few, <u>minority</u> many)   (mostly <u>majority</u> certainly)

(glib <u>timid</u> tiresome)   (fib <u>bold</u> blame)

(<u>foolish</u> ignoramus rude) (<u>wise</u> known discourteous)

The first pair of words on this page causes problems for a great many people, who try to match hour and minute as opposites. Far from being opposites, these are merely different periods of time.

Minute is a homonym. There are two very different ways of pronouncing the word, each of which has a totally different meaning, as in the sentence:

A <u>minute</u> is a <u>minute</u> period of time

- In the first use of the word, it is pronounced 'min-it' and it is a short period of time

- The second time I used the word in the sentence above, you need to pronounce it as 'my-newt' and you have a synonym for miniscule or tiny.

<u>Joke Time!</u>

Although he is not particularly small, I call my pet
amphibian 'Tiny' because he is <u>my newt</u>!

To find out more, go to <u>www.amazon.co.uk</u> and download the
11+ Vocabulary Booster

<u>http://www.amazon.co.uk/11-Vocabulary-Booster-Support-</u>
<u>ebook/dp/B00CEOUOT2/ref=sr_1_2?ie=UTF8&qid=1375667</u>
<u>149&sr=8-2&keywords=11%2B+vocabulary</u>

11+ Guide to Short Writing Tasks

VCOP, Sentence Openers and QAAG

VCOP

In all writing, remember Variety in VCOP is important – But what's it all about?

Vocabulary

Use interesting, ambitious vocabulary wherever possible. Remember: if it's hard to spell, it's good to use! Don't forget a range of amazing adjectives and powerful verbs as well.

Make sure you use metaphors, similes, personification, alliteration etc. in descriptive writing. Can you get some onomatopoeia in there too?

Connectives

Use an interesting range of connectives – not just and, but, then.

Try: - although, whereas, since, whilst, however, because, so, moreover, nevertheless, furthermore etc.

Can you start one of your sentences with 'Although …'?

Don't forget connectives of time in instruction writing.

Openers

Make sure you start your piece of writing in an interesting way. You want to catch the attention of the reader (your audience) from the very beginning! Rhetorical questions can help here.

Try to vary the way you start each sentence in your writing. It's far too easy (and boring!) to start each one with the subject or a subject pronoun.

Try starting with a verb, an adverb or an adverbial clause

Could you start with a preposition or an adjective, or even the object?

Punctuation

Check the accuracy of your basic punctuation – full stops, commas and capital letters.

Make sure you have written at least 2 paragraphs; but don't necessarily leave a line between each one. Use indentation!

Try to use either a question mark or an exclamation mark

Additionally, try to use at least 3 of the following in each piece.

( )	...	-	" "	;	:	's	n't

Openers

It is vitally important to grab the attention of our readers from the moment they start to look at our work. So, how can we do this? The answer is obvious - by starting our writing in an unusual way, we will make them want to read it! When you've done that, you need to keep your reader's attention by keeping the writing lively and varying your sentence starts.

Try not to start with the subject or a subject pronoun every time. This is the most common way of starting a sentence and much of the writing your examiner or marker reads will start in this way.

> Who did it ... what did they do?

> I, She, They, The old lady, Mrs. James   etc.

Here are some alternative ideas (and examples!)
- Start with a question – preferably a rhetorical question.
  - How would you feel if you were to meet a lion? What would you think?
  - What do you think is the most important thing about school? I'll tell you! In my opinion, it is ...
- Start with an adverb or an adverbial phrase – how was the action done? Where did it happen? When did it happen?
  - Quickly, the boy picked up his book and ran out of the room.

- Ponderously, the tortoise plodded down the garden, eying the luscious lettuce in the vegetable patch. Would he get there before he was spotted?
  - Start with an action – preferably an 'ing' word –
    - Running down the hill, she fell over and landed face down in the mud!
    - Chasing its tail, the dog looked like a spinning top – or an unlit, spinning Catherine wheel!
    - Opening the wrapper carefully, I hear the gentle rustling before the aroma escapes, jumping up to bite me on the nose!
    - Squeezing through the tiniest of gaps, she urged herself ever onwards.
  - Start with a preposition.
    - Behind the rock, far away from preying eyes, the tiny mouse sat and waited.
    - Near to where the children played, some strange creature was lurking in its lair; something half-human, half-animal. What could it be?
  - Start with a connective
    - Although everyone knows that monkeys are mischievous, few people are aware of how naughty they can be.
    - Whilst I love all types of fruit, I have to say that by far my favourite is the peach.
    - Moreover …
    - Nevertheless …

- On the other hand …
- As a result …
  - Start with an adjective
    - Small, silver and shiny; the coin lay there, unclaimed.
  - Start with the object, rather than the subject
    - The umbrella which he held in his arms was, perhaps, the only really normal thing about him.
    - The green hat perched precariously on his cheeky, green face made you want to laugh!
  - Start with a comparative or superlative adjective.
    - Smaller than all the other fish in the pond, Goldie darted through the weeds.
    - More urgent than ever was his need to reach home – to reach his mother.
    - The greatest reason has to be …
  - Start with a simile
    - Like a somnolent statue perched on his rock, this majestic beast opened his massive mouth to emit an indolent roar.
    - Like a silver coin emerging from a black, velvet purse, the moon crept out to brighten the countryside.
    - As quiet as a tiny mouse, Emma cautiously emerged from her hiding place. Had he gone? Had he really gone?

QAAG

Another great hint I picked up on a course somewhere is to try to QAAG in every piece of writing if you really want to engage your reader. Across your two 10 minute tasks, try to ensure you have one example of each element of QAAG somewhere.

QAAG stands for:

QUESTION: Usually rhetorical – this is a great way to grab your reader's attention – to make them think about what you are saying. It's a great introduction for instructions and a fantastic conclusion for descriptive writing. It is also an absolute non-negotiable in advert writing!

ADDRESS YOUR READER: - make them feel that you are writing this for them!

- Have you ever wondered…?
- Could you imagine …?
- Close your eyes and picture this scene.
- Try combining this with …
- Imagine these scrumptious flavours mingling on your spoon

ASIDE: (Often written in brackets or between other forms of parenthesis) – this adds a little extra detail to help the reader understand or to help them picture what you are talking about. In instructional writing, you can use it in the ingredients to say what you prefer to use.

GENERALISATION: This is an 'everyone knows' type of statement, which can challenge your reader.

- Everyone thinks they know how to ... but would you like to know the really best way to ...?

- Of course, no-one can resist the cheeky face of a ...

- Everyone loves to spend time on a quiet, peaceful beach, surrounded by ...

- All ten year olds know that the best sweets are ...

Can We Play Maths Today, Please?

Here are three sample chapters which have been adapted from the book to suit trainee 11+ candidates, one of which look at activities with dice, one which looks at activities with playing cards, and one additional chapter which introduces the concept of BIDMAS, which is essential for tackling the 11+ maths papers.

Using Dice

There are a great many games and activities that merely involve use of dice; not just board games and Yahtzee! Obviously, the more dice you use, the more complicated the games are; but the options are virtually limitless.

Two Dice

- Roll two dice and work out the product of the two numbers. Who can score the greatest total?

Three Dice

- Roll three dice and work out the sum of all three. Who can score the largest total?

- Roll two dice and work out their sum to give you your first number. Roll the third die and calculate the product of your two numbers. Who can score the greatest total? What is the highest possible total? How can you work it out?

- Roll three dice and work out the product of the three numbers rolled. Who can score the highest product? (This includes looking at cubed numbers to 6 cubed – which can be tricky, but which often occur on the maths papers)

Four Dice

- Roll four dice and work out the sum of all four. Who can score the largest total?

- Roll two dice and work out their sum to give you your first number. Next, roll the other two and work out their sum to give you your second number. Work out the product of the two numbers. Who can score the greatest total?

- Roll 4 dice; use addition and multiplication to work out the highest possible answer that can be made from your combination of numbers

- Roll all four dice. How many different totals can you make with your four dice in five minutes? Can you use some of the rules of BIDMAS (explained later) to help you?

e.g. you roll...

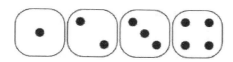

You could score...

1 + 2 + 3 + 4 = 10

1 x 2 x 3 x 4 = 24

(1 + 2) × (3 + 4) = 21

(1 + 2) × 3 × 4 = 36

etc.

Score 1 point for every different total made. Score 20 points to gain a 'reward'.

Year 6 children can use aspects of BIDMAS in their answers, in which case, they may like to check their answers on a scientific calculator.

Six Dice

- Roll all six dice and work out the total sum. Who can score the largest total?

- Roll two dice and work out their sum to give you your first number and multiply it by one of the others. Choose the three of your dice that will give the greatest product and declare it. Who can score the greatest total?

How many different totals can your child make in 5 minutes?

- Choose 3 of your dice and work out their product. Who can score the highest product?

- Mega tricky game! Roll all six dice. How many different totals can you make with your six dice in five minutes?

e.g. you roll...

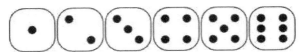

You could score...

1 + 2 + 3 + 4 + 5 + 6 = 21

1 x 2 x 3 x 4 x 5 x 6 = 720

(1 + 2) x (3 + 4) x (5 + 6) = 21 x 11 = 231

Or you could use just a few of your dice

1 + 2 + 3 + 4 = 10

1 x 2 x 3 x 4 = 24

(1 + 2) x (3 + 4) = 21

(1 + 2) x 3 x 4 = 36

etc.

Score 1 point for every different total made and 2 points for the highest total each time. Score 20 points to gain a 'reward'.

11+ candidates and Year 6 children can use aspects of BIDMAS in their answers, in which case, they may like to check their answers on a scientific calculator.

Using Polyhedral Dice

A range of different polyhedral dice can be purchased online, both through Amazon and also through eBay. Use of these widen the range of numbers usable in games and raise the limits infinitely.

Put a set of these down in front of your child from around Years 3/4 after having played a range of dice games and step back. See what they can come up with! Children can be quite ingenious with their ideas; particularly after having been challenged by use of unusual tools!

Using Playing Cards

There are literally hundreds of games that can be played using an ordinary pack of playing games. From simple number matching games such as 'snap' to games which involve more complex mathematical skills, the options are virtually limitless. Many ideas have been included in the year group sections of this book; however, here are a few others that you might like to try.

Snap

Everyone knows this game! Divide the cards equally between the players; then take it in turns to place a card on the pile. When the two top cards match, the first player to shout 'snap' takes the pile. The winner is the player with the most cards at the end of game.

Thirteen

Like 'snap' but this time you shout when the top two cards total 13. In this game, an ace counts as 1, jack as 11, queen as 12 and king as 13 (so wins as a solo card!)

Twenty Four

As above, but this time looking at the <u>product</u> of the top two cards. When the product is 24, shout out!

Because 24 is a number that has a lot of factors, it is a fairly easy total to work towards; however, you might like to change the challenge to other numbers. Any multiple of 12 is good – 36 is very good!

Deal 'em - Adders.

This activity is great for rapid addition work and number bond revision.

Remove all the 'royal' cards from the pack, leaving you with a standard pack of ace to ten cards in the four suits. Shuffle the cards thoroughly and place them face down on the table. Take it in turns to turn over the top card, adding its total to the ones already turned.

e.g. You turn over the 5

Your child turns over the 7 and shouts out '12'

You turn over a 6 – your child shouts '18'

Your child turns over a 3 – '21' etc.

Deal 'em – Subtractors.

Play as above, but subtract from 110

e.g. You turn over the 5. Your child shouts out '105'

Your child turns over the 7 and shouts out '98'

You turn over a 6 – your child shouts '92'

Your child turns over a 3 – '89' etc.

Deal 'em Positive and negative

This is a game for children from the top of Year 4 into years 5 and 6.

Just like the previous games, remove the 'royal' cards from your hand first, then shuffle the cards and place them in a pile in the centre of the table. Turn them over, one at a time. In this version of the game, however, black cards are 'positive' – so you add those. Red cards are negative – so their scores are subtracted from the total.

If played correctly, your final total should be 0; although you should pass through a range of negative numbers in the process.

Once your child gets good at this, you might like to 'fiddle' the shuffle to ensure that 3 or 4 red cards are encountered in a row, ensuring the use of negative totals – if you think you can get away with a bit of simple cheating!

Jubilee

A game for between 2 & 8 players (although for more than 4 players, I recommend the use of 2 packs of cards).

Starting with a full set of cards, shuffle them carefully and place them in the centre of the table.

One player turns over the cards, mentally adding each number to the previous total until a Royal card (Jack, Queen or King) is turned – at which point, the opponents shout 'Jubilee'. Their score is frozen and written down before the turn is passed to the next player.

If they get another go, they continue from their previous total.

The winner is the one who has reached the highest total once the last card has been turned.

Variations on this Game

Whilst at the earlier stages, you might like to shout 'Jubilee' for every Royal card; once your child becomes more confident, you may want to save this purely for Kings.

Jubilee Plus & Jubilee Minus.

Starting with a full set of cards, shuffle them carefully and place them in the centre of the table.

In this version of the game, red cards are all negative; whereas black cards are always positive.

One player turns over the cards, adding or subtracting each number to/from the previous total until a Royal card is turned – at which point, the opponents shout 'Jubilee'. Their score is frozen and written down before the turn is passed to the next player.

If they get another go, they continue from their previous total.

The winner is the one who has reached the highest total once the last card has been turned.

Variation on this Game

Whilst at the earlier stages, you might like to shout 'Jubilee' for every Royal card; once your child becomes more confident, you may want to save this purely for Kings, which results in speedier play.

Deal 'em Tables.

Take a pack of cards and remove all the 'Royals'. Shuffle well and place upside down on the table. Take it in turns to turn over the top card and multiply it to the one previously on top, calling out the product of the two.

e.g. You turn over the 5

Your child turns over a 7 and calls out ' $5 \times 7 = 35$ '

You turn over a 4 – ' $7 \times 4 = 28$ '

Your child turns over an 8 – '4 x 8 = 32'

You turn over a 6 – '6 x 8 = 48'

Etc.

If your child is good at this, introduce the 'Royals' so that a jack is 11, a Queen is 12 and a King is 13; then play as above.

To make it really hard, try making the red cards negative numbers and the black cards positive. What do they do when they turn 2 red cards over? What happens with a red card and a black one? Is it always the same?

<u>Twenty-one</u>

This is a simplified version of the casino game, without the gambling involved. Deal 2 cards to your child and two to yourself. They look at their cards and add up the total, deciding whether any Ace in their hand counts as a 1 or 11. All other 'royal' cards count as 10. They then decide whether to stick (keep their current total) or twist (risk taking another card). You then turn your cards over. The player whose total is nearest to, but not exceeding, 21 is the winner and scores a point. Anyone who has scored exactly 21 scores 2 points. Score 3 points if you have managed it in 2 cards. Set a target number of points for the end of the match and stick to it.

Regal Twenty-one

Make '21' more complex by counting the 'Royal' cards as: jack = 11; Queen = 12; King = 13. Score as above.

BIDMAS

As you will have noticed from the sections above, by Years 5 & 6, your child will be moving on to some quite difficult aspects of maths; one of the trickiest of which is BIDMAS (sometimes also referred to as BODMAS). This is a concept that often catches parents out, as well as children. Frequently, I have parents ask me why the answer to a question is wrong, and then I find myself having to explain BIDMAS to them as well!

Here is a brief explanation of what BIDMAS is all about for those of you who are unsure.

First of all, however, try this sum

$$4 + 6 \times 8 =$$

If you said 52; well done! You clearly already know what BIDMAS is. If, however, your response was 80 and you can't see where I got my answer of 52 from; don't worry. You are not alone, but you will need to read the explanation below!

This type of problem catches a lot of people out, and a normal calculator will also give you the faulty answer of 80 for this particular question. The reason is that it is incapable of sorting the whole sum and so dealing the relative parts of the problem in the correct order. If you try the same sum on a scientific calculator, you will see that it believes that the answer should be 52, because it doesn't solve the problem as you input each section and so is able to apply the rules of BIDMAS; which state the order of any calculation should be:

- Brackets – these should always be solved first, wherever they might appear in the sum

- Indices or Powers Of – e.g. 5^2. These should be solved next, regardless of where they appear in the sum.

- Division & Multiplication. These are solved next; but this time, they are solved in the order that they appear in the sum.

- Addition & Subtraction. When only addition and subtraction are left, start from the left hand side and work through them in the order in which they appear in the sum.

In other words, you should always multiply BEFORE adding; even if the addition looks to come first in the sum.

6 x 8 = 48 + 4 = 52. (An answer of 80 is usually described as being a BADMIS in my class, for more reasons than one!)

Example 2

What is 4 + 5 x 3?

In BIDMAS, multiplication comes before addition, so multiply 5 by 3 first.

4 + 5 × 3 = 4 + 15 = 19, so this is the right answer.

(27 is a BADMIS – you have added before multiplying.)

If you think you are beginning to understand this tricky concept, have a go at the examples below; then look at my answers and explanations on the following pages.

Check your understanding here!

Using BIDMAS, can you work out the value of the following?

(Answers and explanations are on the next page.)

a) 4 × 5 - 3 × 2

b) (2 + 3) × (5 - 1)

c) 2 + 6 ÷ 2

d) 8 - (6 - 1)

e) 3 × (4 + 2)

f) $4 + 5 \times 12 - 7^2$

g) $(4 + 5) \times 12 - 7^2$

Answers and explanation:

a) 4 x 5 + 3 x 2 = 14.

In BIDMAS multiplication comes before subtraction, so you should work out the multiplication first and then do the subtraction in order to get the correct answer:
4 × 5 - 3 × 2 = 20 - 6 = 14

b) (2 + 3) x (5 − 1) = 20

Solve the brackets first, so that the working is

(2 + 3) = 5; (5 - 1) = 4; 5 × 4 = 20

c) 2 + 6 ÷ 2 = 5

In BIDMAS division comes before addition, so

2 + 6 ÷ 2 = 2 + 3 = 5

d) 8 − (6 − 1) = 3

Brackets come first, so

8 - (6 - 1) = 8 - 5 = 3

e) 3 x (4 + 2) = 18

BIDMAS states that brackets come before multiplication, so work out the bracket first:

(4 + 2) = 6, so

3 × (4 + 2) = 3 × 6 = 18

f) $4 + 5 \times 12 - 7^2 = 15$

First come the indices. **7^2 is 49**.

Next comes the multiplication. **5 × 12 = 60**

You now have the sum **4 + 60 − 49**

4 + 60 = 64. 64 − 49 = 15

g) $(4 + 5) \times 12 - 7^2 = 59$

Brackets come first. **4 + 5 = 9**

Indices come next. 7^2 **= 49**

This is followed by the multiplication. **9 × 12 = 108**

Finally, you can tackle the subtraction.

108 − 49 = 59

Printed in Great Britain
by Amazon